NIHAR HARI

Ten Cents of Hope

A youth's guide to never living paycheck-to-paycheck

First published by Ten Cents of Hope 2026

Library of Congress Control Number: 2026915112.

This work contains AI-generated illustrations. The text is the original work of the author.

First edition

ISBN: 979-8-9965650-0-9

This book was professionally typeset on Reedsy.
Find out more at reedsy.com

Contents

Foreword v
Acknowledgments vii
Introduction 1

I THE SEED

1 What we know and what nobody told us 5
2 Money Is a Language 7
3 Where Does Money Actually Go? 9

II THE ROOTS

4 Our First Dollar 15
5 The Magic of Time 17
6 Debt Is Not the Enemy 19
7 Budgeting Without the Misery 21
8 The Brain vs. The Wallet 25
9 Investing Isn't Just for Rich People 28
10 Making Money 31

III THE FRUIT

11 Goals, Not Dreams 37
12 The Privilege Gap 40

13 Building Our Circle 42

IV REPLANTING

14 The Ten Cent Action Plan 47

V Glossary

15 Commonly Used Terms In This Book 57

About the Author 61

Foreword

By Dr. Michael Pearson

At The Carying Place, we have taught financial literacy to working families experiencing homelessness for over thirty years. Our work spans all ages, from parents learning to budget and build credit, to the children and teenagers watching their families rebuild while forming their own relationship with money. We believe breaking the cycle of generational homelessness means reaching the next generation before the crisis reaches them.

Nihar first came to us as a volunteer, wanting to teach financial literacy to the youth in our Children and Teens Program. He showed up, led sessions, and connected with our young people in a way that was immediately evident—genuinely invested in every person in the room.

When I learned more about Ten Cents of Hope, Nihar's nonprofit, and the work he was already doing around youth financial literacy, it was clear his mission aligned with what we see young people need every day. From those early conversations, and through months of close collaboration, this book took shape. I reviewed chapter outlines, content, and drafts throughout, and I can say honestly that what Nihar brought to each revision—the willingness to rethink, to listen, to push further—is what separates this book from everything else I have seen in this space.

What makes Ten Cents of Hope valuable for programs like ours is something no adult educator can manufacture: the voice of a peer. The teenagers in our program are navigating one of the hardest chapters of their family's life. They are perceptive—they know when they're being talked down to, and when someone is speaking honestly from genuine care. Nihar's voice here is the latter: direct, warm, and respectful of the reader's intelligence, which is exactly what these young people deserve.

The families I work with are proof of what happens when financial knowledge arrives too late. This book is proof of what's possible when it arrives early, from someone who understands what young people need to hear, and how.

Dr. Michael Pearson

Director of Programs, The Carying Place

Ph.D., Philosophy in Health and Human Services, UNCG & NCAT

Cary, North Carolina

Acknowledgments

This book was created with the mentorship and guidance of Dr. Michael Pearson, Director at The Carying Place. The Carying Place is a 501(c)(3) non-profit that teaches homeless working families with children financial literacy and other life skills to attain independent living.

I would like to acknowledge **Dr. Michael Pearson** for his support and guidance throughout the creation of this book. This project didn't come from one person. It grew out of conversations, questions, mistakes, and small wins shared with Dr. Pearson. Every chapter carries pieces of his voice and encouragement, shaped by his knowledge and experience in the field.

To Dr. Pearson: THANK YOU for the weekly meetings, the words of wisdom, and the honesty that pushed this project forward more than you know.

Thank you for testing ideas with me, challenging my thinking, and sharing your own experiences with financial literacy. This book is stronger because of your perspective.

You were truly a mentor, teacher, coach, and leader. Thank you for modeling what responsibility, generosity, and patience look like. You taught me that financial wisdom isn't about being perfect; it's about being willing to learn and willing to share.

Thank you for taking the time to review drafts, offer feedback, and say "Keep going" when it mattered most. Your support turned scattered notes into something whole. You helped me believe this book could matter.

And finally, thank you for helping *Ten Cents of Hope* become more than an idea or a book. It is a community, a mindset, and a reminder that small steps can change everything. This is our pomegranate.

Introduction

I wrote this for anyone between 13 and 18 who has ever watched money disappear and wondered where it went — whether you've had your first job, your first paycheck, or just your first birthday card with cash in it.

This is my story. This is why I started Ten Cents of Hope. I thought getting my first paycheck would feel amazing. But after taxes and buying the things I needed, most of it was already gone. That's when I realized how fast money disappears. And when I looked around, I noticed something else: most of my friends, smart and driven as they are, never learned how money even works, either at school or at home.

Here is something I realized about the adult world, that most people run out of money before their next paycheck. Realizing adults don't have everything figured out, or seeing the stress parents have about bills, rent, or groceries, learning a friend is working a job to help their family, and realizing life isn't fair, and effort doesn't always equal outcome. These stories became a wake-up moment.

So, here's my promise: I'm not going to talk down to you. I realize you don't need to be rich to start learning this stuff. I'm a teenager, writing this for other kids. No lectures, and no fancy words. Just someone trying to figure things out and sharing what I've learned along the way.

I

THE SEED

Seeing money clearly for the first time

Let me be real: we don't all start in the same place. I was lucky; my parents talked about money at the dinner table. But a lot of my friends never had those conversations. By the time we finish high school, some kids have already seen how investing works or had accounts opened for them. That kind of head start is real. But learning about money isn't a race.

1

What we know and what nobody told us

Ever crack open a pomegranate? Inside, there are hundreds of tiny seeds. Each one looks small, but together they fill the whole fruit. Money works the same way. Every little thing you learn is another seed. This part of the book is about seeing money clearly for the first time, not as a math problem, not as something to stress over, but as a skill. A skill **most of us never learned,** but all of us **need to know**.

Think about what it means to learn a language as a kid versus as an adult. Kids pick it up effortlessly because they're surrounded by it, they're not afraid to make mistakes, and they have time to let it sink in. That's exactly where you are with money right now. You haven't made the big mistakes yet. You haven't signed a lease you couldn't afford, taken out a loan you didn't understand, or said yes to a credit card because it came with a free t-shirt. You're still in the learning phase. And that means you get to build the right habits before the stakes are high.

Most adults learned about money the hard way: trial and error, usually after it cost them something real, like a bounced check or a missed payment. A credit score that took years to rebuild. They wish someone had sat them down at 15 and explained how this all works. This book is that conversation. And the fact that you're reading it at all means you're already ahead of where most people started.

Notes

2

Money Is a Language

I used to think money was just math: numbers, charts, boring stuff. But it's really more like a language; a whole system of words and rules. I didn't know what a credit score was until I was 14. Compound interest? I had no idea.

But here's the good news: if money wasn't talked about much at home, it's not too late to learn the money language.

When I first started learning about money, I kept hearing adults say things like, "You don't want to fall behind." That sounded scary... until I realized something important: being behind at 15 is nothing like being behind at 35. At our age, it's more like showing up to a game a few minutes late; you can still jump in, catch up, and even get ahead.

Right now, time is on your side. You have this huge open window to learn, try things, and make mistakes without it ruining your life. That's honestly why I wrote this book. I wanted other kids to know that starting now is a superpower, not a problem.

Notes

3

Where Does Money Actually Go?

The Truth About Spending

Every adult loves to hit us with the "**needs vs. wants**" lecture. And sure, that's part of it. But the real problem? I had no idea where my money was actually going. Like, I'd get $50 for my birthday, and two weeks later, it was all gone. $5 on a drink here, $12 on something random here and there. At the end of the week? Nothing left. Sound familiar?

I started paying attention to what I call **unconscious** spending; the stuff we don't even realize we're doing. We see something on Instagram, we click, we buy. A friend gets a new hoodie, and suddenly we need one too. It's not about feeling guilty. It's about noticing the **pattern**.

When I first started learning about money, I decided to try something simple. I told myself, "Okay, for one week, I'm going to write down every single thing I spend money on." I didn't change anything. I didn't try to be perfect. I just kept track.

And honestly, I was shocked. I thought I barely spent anything, but seeing it all written out made me realize where my money was really going. It felt like turning on a light in a dark room. Suddenly, everything made sense.

That's why I think everyone should try it. One week. No judging yourself. Just noticing. You might be surprised, too.

Here's something that made it even easier for me: I stopped thinking about it as budgeting and started thinking about it as just paying attention. Budgeting sounds like a restriction, but paying attention sounds like curiosity. And curiosity is a lot easier to maintain than discipline.

The other thing I noticed was how much of my spending was invisible. Not because I was hiding it from myself, but because it happened in such small increments that none of it felt significant in the moment. A dollar here, three dollars there. The problem isn't any single purchase. The problem is that those small purchases never feel like a decision. They feel like nothing. And when you add up a hundred 'nothings,' you end up with an empty wallet and a lot of confusion about where it all went.

That one week of tracking changed how I saw every purchase after it. Not because I stopped buying things I wanted, but because I started making those purchases on purpose. That shift from unconscious to intentional is honestly one of the most valuable things in this entire book.

Notes

II

THE ROOTS

Habits, saving, and the systems that hold everything up

Habits and systems are like the hidden foundation that holds everything together. Think about a pomegranate tree. The fruit doesn't just pop out one day. Before anything grows, the roots have to push deep into the ground. You don't see them. They're not exciting. But they're the reason the tree survives storms, dry seasons, and time.

4

Our First Dollar

How to Save When It Feels Like There's Nothing to Save

I've heard this so many times. "I don't make enough to save." I used to say it myself. But here's what I found out: saving isn't about having a lot of money. It's about building those money muscles. It's a habit, not about how much you have.

The trick that changed everything for me: save a percentage, not a fixed number. Got $20 for a birthday? Put $2 aside. That's 10%. That's the **ten-cent mindset**: small actions that add up over time. It doesn't matter if the money came from a job, an allowance, a birthday card, or mowing lawns. What matters is starting now.

Notes

5

The Magic of Time

And Why Starting at 16 Beats Starting at 30

This is the chapter that honestly changed my whole perspective. When I first understood compound interest, I couldn't believe nobody had told me sooner. It's the most powerful idea in personal finance. And the earlier you start, the harder it works for you.

Let me lay out the numbers; they're wild:

Imagine putting away just $50 a month starting at 16, earning an average annual return of 7%, a conservative long-term estimate for a diversified index fund. That one small habit could grow to around $40,000 by your early 40s, over $50,000 by your mid-40s, more than $100,000 by your mid-50s, and roughly a quarter million dollars by retirement age. The math isn't magic; it's time. And right now, you have more of it than almost anyone else around you.

Notes

6

Debt Is Not the Enemy

Misunderstanding debt and not using it to our advantage is to our detriment.

Everyone talks about debt like it's this scary monster we should avoid at all costs. But that's not the full picture. Some debt actually helps us: a student loan that gets you a degree, a mortgage on a home. Other debt traps: high-interest credit cards, predatory lending, and those buy-now-pay-later traps that seem harmless until they're not. Learning the difference changed how I saw everything.

When I first started learning about money, I realized something nobody had ever said out loud: most of us meet debt long before we ever meet investing. Especially if you grow up in a household where money is tight, debt shows up early, sometimes before you even understand what it is. Debt isn't automatically bad; it's a tool. A tool can help you or hurt you depending on how you use it. Take credit scores, for example. A credit score is basically a number that shows how responsibly you handle borrowed money. One of the biggest parts of that score is something called *utilization*: how much of your available credit you're actually using. Keeping that number low tells lenders you're managing things well.

Learning this before 18 doesn't mean you need a credit card right now. It just means you'll understand the rules of the game before you ever have to play it. And when you understand the tool, you're far less likely to get trapped by it.

Notes

7

Budgeting Without the Misery

How to Spend With Purpose, Not Guilt

Let's be real, though: budgeting sounds boring. Restrictive. Like something our parents would make us do. I thought the same thing. But once I actually tried it, I realized a budget isn't a cage. It's freedom. It's not about spending less. It's about spending with purpose.

That's where the Ten Cents of Hope system comes in. It starts small—literally with a dime out of every dollar—but it grows into a whole way of thinking about money. And it actually works for teenagers, especially when our income is random and unpredictable.

Consider a dime out of every dollar. It sounds tiny, almost too small to matter, but that's exactly the point. Giving a little is like tapping the brakes on the idea that money defines you. If you get $100 for your birthday, $10 goes to someone or something that matters to you. Simple. But the habit it builds—remembering that money is a tool, not your identity—is what stays with you.

From there, save 30%. This is your "future-you" stash. Not the kind of savings you raid for new shoes or a last-minute snack run. This is the quiet pile you treat as untouchable, the part that grows in the background. And here's why it's 30% instead of the usual 20% adults talk about: right now, we don't pay rent. We don't buy groceries. We don't cover insurance. This is the one moment in life when saving big barely hurts, so we take advantage of it.

Then take 20%. This is where the long game begins. This bucket is for the tools that help your money grow while you sleep: things like a custodial brokerage or a Roth IRA. And if you're not ready for all that yet, that's okay. Start this bucket at zero and let it grow as you learn. The point isn't perfection. It's planting a seed early enough that time does most of the work for you.

And if you want to spend freely, take 40%. This is the part that makes the whole system feel human. Forty cents of every dollar is yours to enjoy however you want. No guilt. No tracking. No adult hovering over your shoulder. This is your fun money; the part that makes the other 60% feel doable instead of suffocating. Freedom is built into the plan on purpose.

That's the Ten Cents of Hope plan: a simple system that turns every dollar into a chance to build something better, without making your life miserable.

Let me walk through what this actually looks like in real life. Say you make $200 in a month from a part-time job, some lawn work, or a combination of both. Here's how the Ten Cents of Hope split works:

Give: $20 (10%)

This goes to something that matters: Ten Cents of Hope, a local food bank, a friend's fundraiser, whatever resonates with you. The amount doesn't matter as much as the habit of giving before you spend. It rewires how you think about money, from something you hoard to something you circulate.

Save: $60 (30%)

This is your untouchable pile. Put it in a savings account separate from your checking account, ideally one you can't see easily on your phone. Out of sight, out of mind. Let it sit. This is future-you's money, and future-you will be grateful.

Invest: $40 (20%)

If you have a custodial account set up, this goes in there. If you don't yet, put it in savings for now and label it 'investing fund.' When you're ready to open an account, it'll already be waiting. Don't skip this bucket just because you're not sure how to invest yet. Start saving it first, learn second.

Spend: $80 (40%)

This is yours, no explanation needed. Snacks, movies, a new hoodie, whatever. Spend it freely and without guilt. The whole point of the other 60% is to make this 40% feel genuinely guilt-free. You've already done the responsible part. Enjoy the rest.

The numbers will change as your income changes. When you're earning $2,000 a month instead of $200, the percentages stay the same, but the amounts grow. The habit is the thing. The amounts follow the habit.

Notes

8

The Brain vs. The Wallet

Why Smart People Make Dumb Money Decisions

This might be my favorite chapter to talk about, because it applies to literally all of us. It doesn't matter if we have $20 or $20,000; our brains are wired to be bad with money. Mine included. Once I learned why, everything clicked.

Like, why does losing $20 feel so much worse than finding $20 feels good? Why would I rather have $50 right now than $100 in a year, even though the math is obvious? Why do I suddenly want something I didn't care about five minutes ago, just because my friend has it? The sneakers. The phone. The outfit you didn't even want until you saw it on someone's story.

I'm not saying you should stop wanting things. That's not realistic. That's not even the point. The point is understanding why you want them, and then making the call on purpose instead of on impulse.

There's a name for what's happening in your brain when you see something and immediately want it: loss aversion and social comparison, two of the most well-documented biases in behavioral economics. Loss aversion means we feel losses about twice as strongly as we feel equivalent gains. That's why losing $20 feels so much worse than finding $20 feels good — even though mathematically, they're identical. Social comparison means we constantly measure ourselves against the people around us. When your friend gets something new, your brain registers it as you falling behind, even when you weren't even thinking about it five minutes ago.

Neither of these is a character flaw. They're features of a brain that evolved to keep us safe and connected in communities.

The problem is that those instincts were designed for a world without Instagram, without influencer marketing, without stores engineered by teams of psychologists to make you want things you never knew you needed. The environment has changed faster than our brains have.

So what do you actually do with this? A few things that helped me: First, the 48-hour rule. If I want something that costs more than I'd normally spend on a snack, I wait 48 hours before buying it. Nine times out of ten, the urge fades completely. Second, I turned off one-click purchasing everywhere I shop online. Adding friction to the purchase process breaks the impulse cycle. Third, I started asking myself one question before any non-essential purchase: 'Am I buying this because I want it, or because I saw someone else have it?' That one question has saved me more money than any budget spreadsheet.

Notes

9

Investing Isn't Just for Rich People

It's How People Become Less Poor

I used to think investing was for other people. Adults in suits.

Stockbrokers. Six-figure salaries. Not for a teenager with birthday money and a part-time job. I was totally wrong. And I don't want you making the same mistake I did.

A teenager can start investing through something called a **custodial account**, which is an account an adult opens for you, but the money inside belongs to you. It gives you a legal way to invest before you turn 18, and it's the doorway to future investing.

Inside a custodial account, you can buy things like **index funds**. An index fund is simply a bundle of hundreds of companies in one place, so instead of trying to guess which company will win, you own a tiny piece of all of them at once. This makes investing less risky and a lot easier to understand.

You can also buy **ETFs**, which are basically index funds you can purchase for the price of a sandwich. ETFs let you start with very small amounts (even $5) and still own a piece of the whole market. They're simple, flexible, and beginner-friendly, which makes them perfect for teens who want to learn without putting in a lot of money.

The reason all of this is significant is that **time** is the real superpower. When you start investing as a teenager, even tiny amounts have decades to grow. You don't need to pick the "right" stock or become a financial expert. You just need to understand the tools and start small.

And one thing to be clear about: this chapter isn't about recommending specific stocks or funds. That's what financial advisors are for. What we're doing here is learning the concepts so that when the time comes, you actually know what you're looking at and what questions to ask.

Here's the most practical thing I can tell you about getting started: open a custodial account with Fidelity, Schwab, or Vanguard. All three have no minimum balance requirements and no account fees. Your parent or guardian opens it with you as the beneficiary, and you can begin investing immediately. When you turn 18, the account transfers to you automatically.

Once the account is open, start with an index fund that tracks the S&P 500, something like FXAIX at Fidelity, SWTSX at Schwab, or VTSAX at Vanguard. These funds give you exposure to hundreds of American companies in a single investment. You don't need to pick stocks. You don't need to watch the market every day. You just need to put money in consistently and leave it alone.

Here's the part that trips people up: the market goes down sometimes. It went down in 2008. It went down in 2020. It will go down again. When it does, the worst thing you can do is panic and sell. The best thing you can do is keep buying, because you're getting the same investment at a lower price. This mindset, called dollar-cost averaging, is one of the most powerful tools available to a young investor. And the earlier you develop it, the more naturally it becomes your instinct during the inevitable bad stretches.

Notes

10

Making Money

Jobs, Side Hustles, and the Gig Economy

Let's talk about actually making money. Not theory, not inspiration, just real options that work at 15, 16, or 17 with no car, no startup capital, and no business degree.

Trading Time for Money (The Starting Point)

The first kind of income is simple: you have a skill or your time, someone needs it, and they pay you. This includes babysitting, lawn care, pet sitting, tutoring, lifeguarding, retail jobs, and food service. These aren't glamorous, but they're real money with real hours. The key insight here is to treat these jobs like school: show up on time, do the work better than asked, and build a reputation. In a neighborhood or small community, your reputation spreads faster than any social media post. One good reference from a satisfied client or employer leads to three more.

If you go this route, track your hours and your income from day one. Even if you're getting paid cash. This builds the habit of treating your earnings like a business, not just pocket money. And if you ever need to report income or apply for financial aid, you'll already have records.

Skill-Based Freelancing

If you can do something that others can't—or can't do as well—you can charge for it. Graphic design, video editing, photography, social media management, tutoring in a specific subject, coding, writing, music lessons, and translation. These services are in genuine demand, and being a teenager is actually an advantage in some of them. Businesses and nonprofits often specifically want someone young who understands how social media actually works.

Start by offering your service to one or two people for free or at a steep discount in exchange for an honest review or testimonial. Once you have proof of results, you can charge real rates. Post your availability in local Facebook groups, Nextdoor, and through school bulletin boards. You don't need a website to start; you need a phone number and a willingness to do good work.

Reselling

Buy low, sell high. This is one of the oldest business models in existence, and it's fully accessible to teenagers. Thrift stores, garage sales, and estate sales are full of undervalued items. Vintage clothing, sneakers, sports cards, video games, and books are among the most reliable categories. Learn what sells on eBay, Depop, or Facebook Marketplace in your area. Start with $20 and see what you can flip. The skills you build, such as spotting value, negotiating, writing a compelling listing, and managing customer communication, are the same skills that drive billion-dollar businesses.

Content Creation (The Long Game)

YouTube, TikTok, Instagram. These are legitimate income sources, but they take time. The mistake most people make is expecting results in weeks instead of months. If you're genuinely interested in creating content, start now and commit to consistency for at least 6 months before evaluating whether it's working. Pick one platform. Pick one topic you actually care about. Post regularly. Engage with your audience. The creator economy is real, but it rewards patience and authenticity more than luck or equipment.

The Most Important Lesson About Earning

Here's what nobody tells you: the goal isn't just to make money. It's to learn what it feels like to earn money, to make decisions with money you worked for, and to understand the difference between trading your time and building something that creates value on its own. Every dollar you earn as a teenager teaches you something that no class or book can fully replicate. So take the job. Start the side hustle. Sell the thing. Not because you need the money right now, but because the person you're becoming needs the experience.

Notes

III

THE FRUIT

Goals, independence, and what we're actually building toward

The pomegranate is the part people notice; that deep red, impossible-to-ignore result of everything that grew beneath the surface. But crack it open, and we realize the fruit was never one big thing. It's hundreds of small seeds, held together.

11

Goals, Not Dreams

How to Actually Get What We Want

There's a big difference between "I want to be rich" and "I want to save $2,000 for a car by next June." One is a dream. The other is a goal. I learned this the hard way; I spent a long time wanting things without ever making a real plan to get them.

What we're doing in this section is learning how to turn those vague wants into something real. We're going to look at short-term, medium-term, and long-term goals, and the resources you need to achieve them. Now, what we should keep in mind is that the goal(s) you choose should matter to *you*; many of my goals in the past were made because others wanted to see me reach them, even though I didn't really care as much about the goal. The goal should matter to you: maybe it's saving for a car so you don't have to ask for rides anymore. Maybe it's a trip with friends, or putting money aside for college, or building the freedom to move out someday. When your money is tied to something real, something you can picture and feel, saving stops being a chore. It becomes progress; a step toward independence, toward options, toward the version of your life you're trying to build.

A goal without a timeline is just a wish. So here's a simple framework I started using that actually works. For every financial goal, write down three things: what you want, how much it costs, and when you want it by. Then do the math backward. If you want $500 in four months and you're starting from zero, you need to save $125 a month, or about $30 a week. Suddenly, it's not an abstract goal; it's a number you can hit or miss every single week. That clarity changes everything.

Short-term goals (under 3 months) keep you motivated and give you quick wins. A new piece of equipment, a concert ticket, a contribution to a friend's birthday gift. These are the goals that build the savings muscle, because the timeline is short enough to stay real.

Medium-term goals (3 months to a year) are where real financial maturity starts. Saving for a car, a class, a trip, or a meaningful investment. These require actual discipline over actual time, which is exactly what makes achieving them so satisfying.

Long-term goals (1 year and beyond) are where compound interest starts to do the heavy lifting. College savings. An investment portfolio. A down payment on something big. You don't need to have these figured out right now, but having even a rough idea of what you're building toward changes how you make decisions today.

Notes

12

The Privilege Gap

And How to Close It

I want to be real about something. Some of us start with

advantages. I did. My parents talked about money. They opened accounts for me. I had access to information and mentors that a lot of my friends didn't. That gap is real, and I'm not going to pretend it doesn't exist.

But this chapter isn't about feeling bad or sorry for yourself. It's about showing what's available to everyone, right now, for free. Because the gap is real, but the tools to close it are out there. Nobody just told us.

Here are the free resources I wish every teen knew about:

Roth IRAs through Fidelity, Schwab, or Vanguard have no minimum balance and no fees. A parent can open a custodial brokerage account with zero dollars. Khan Academy's Personal Finance course is free and actually great. Investopedia explains every financial term in plain language. The public library has books that change how we think about money. YouTube channels like Two Cents by PBS offer quality financial education in a format teens already use. Google Sheets or free budgeting apps work as well as anything expensive. And FAFSA (the Free Application for Federal Student Aid) is one of the most important and most overlooked tools for teens from lower-income households.

Notes

13

Building Our Circle

Why Who We Learn From Matters

Where you get your financial advice matters just as much as the advice itself. I learned this after going down some rabbit holes on TikTok and YouTube that sounded smart but were basically just people selling courses. They spoke with confidence, used big words, and promised fast results, but none of it was built on real experience. The wrong advice can cost you time, money, and confidence. The right circle can change your life.

That's why learning to spot red flags is a skill. The so-called "gurus" who make their money selling advice instead of following it. The influencers who promise you'll get rich quickly if you just buy their program. The people whose entire business model depends on your fear, your confusion, or your desperation. They're loud, they're everywhere, and they're good at sounding legit. But once you know what to look for, you start to see the patterns: the pressure tactics, the unrealistic promises, the "secret strategies" that somehow always cost $49.99.

Just as important as spotting the wrong voices is finding the right ones. Real mentors don't promise shortcuts. They don't make you feel stupid. They don't try to sell you something every five minutes. They teach, they guide, and they help you think for yourself. Sometimes they're teachers, coaches, older friends, or family members. Sometimes, they're people online who share real knowledge without asking for your credit card. And sometimes they're peers; other teens who are learning, saving, and building alongside you.

That's part of what Ten Cents of Hope is meant to be. Not just a book, but a community. A place where you can learn the basics, ask questions without feeling judged, and build a circle of people who are genuinely good with money, not because they're rich, but because they're responsible, thoughtful, and honest. When you surround yourself with people like that, everything gets easier. You make better choices. You avoid traps. You grow faster. And you start to see money not as something scary or confusing, but as something you can actually control.

Here's a practical way to start building that circle right now: find one adult in your life—a parent, a teacher, a coach, a family friend—who seems genuinely good with money. Not rich. Good with money. Those are very different things. Rich people aren't always good with money. People who are good with money have a calm relationship with it. They don't stress about it constantly, but they also don't ignore it. They know where their money goes. Ask that person if you can ask them a few questions sometime. Most adults who are good at something are genuinely happy to talk about it if someone asks sincerely.

That one conversation could teach you more than a semester of classes. And it might open a door to an ongoing relationship with someone who can help you navigate the decisions that are coming in the next few years: college, first jobs, first credit cards, first apartment. Having a trusted adult you can ask, "Does this make sense?" is one of the most underrated financial advantages a young person can have.

Notes

IV

REPLANTING

Passing it on and breaking the cycle for good

The best thing I can do with what I've learned is to pass it on. Breaking the paycheck-to-paycheck cycle happens when knowledge spreads friend to friend, generation to generation. Replanting means giving seeds back to the next person: a friend, a sibling, a classmate who's never heard money doesn't have to be a source of stress. You don't need to be an expert. This book is one conversation—what you do with it decides how many more happen.

14

The Ten Cent Action Plan

Start Today, Not Someday

Here it is. Thirty days. One small action each day. Nothing on this list requires money you don't have, skills you haven't built, or time you can't find. Each action is designed to be completed in under 30 minutes. By the end of the month, you won't just know more; you'll have actually done the things. And doing is the only thing that sticks.

Week 1: See Clearly

Day 1: Track every dollar you spend today.

Write it down in your phone's notes app or on paper. Every single thing, no matter how small. This is just observation; no judgment, no changes. Just data.

Day 2: Add up yesterday's spending.

Look at your list from Day 1. Categorize it: food, entertainment, transportation, random. How much did you spend in total? Does it surprise you?

Day 3: Find your biggest money leak.

Look back at the last two weeks of spending; check your bank app, Venmo history, or just try to recall. Where is most of your money actually going? Name it.

Day 4: Write down your three most common spending triggers.

Boredom? Social pressure? A specific app? Scrolling? Be honest. Knowing your triggers is the first step to making intentional choices instead of automatic ones.

Day 5: Calculate your monthly income.

Add up every source: job, allowance, gigs, birthday money average. Even if it's inconsistent, get a rough number. This is your starting point.

Day 6: Write your Ten Cents of Hope budget.

Using your income number from Day 5, calculate your Give/Save/Invest/Spend split. Write the actual dollar amounts for each bucket. This is your personal financial plan.

Day 7: Rest and reflect.

Look at what you've learned this week. What surprised you? What do you want to change? Write two sentences about it. This is the practice of financial self-awareness.

Week 2: Build the Foundation

Day 8: Open or review your savings account.

If you don't have one, research your options today. Most banks offer teen savings accounts with no fees. If you already have one, log in and note your balance. This is your home base.

Day 9: Set up a separate 'savings only' account if possible.

Keeping savings in a different account from your spending money removes temptation. Even if it's at the same bank, a separate account creates psychological distance that helps.

Day 10: Make your first intentional transfer.

Move whatever your 30% savings amount is from Day 6 into your savings account. Even if it's $5. This is the habit, not the amount.

Day 11: Learn what a credit score is.

Spend 15 minutes on Investopedia or Khan Academy reading about credit scores. Understand the five factors: payment history, utilization, length of history, new credit, and credit mix. You don't need credit yet. You just need to understand the game before you play it.

Day 12: Look up your state's minimum wage and calculate an hourly living budget.

If you worked 20 hours a week at minimum wage, what would your monthly income be? What could you afford? This exercise builds realistic expectations about money and work.

Day 13: Research one legitimate side hustle you could actually start.

Look up what it takes to get started. What do you need? How long until you'd earn your first dollar? Don't do it yet; just research it thoroughly.

Day 14: Write down your three financial goals.

One short-term (under 3 months), one medium-term (3-12 months), one long-term (1+ years). For each one, write the target amount and your target date. Use the framework from Chapter 3.

Week 3: Go Deeper

Day 15: Watch one personal finance video.

Try Two Cents on YouTube (PBS), Caleb Hammer, or The Plain Bagel. Pick one video, watch it fully, and write down one thing you learned.

Day 16: Ask a trusted adult one money question.

A parent, a teacher, a coach, a family friend. Ask something real: 'What do you wish you'd known about money at my age?' or 'What's one money mistake you'd take back?' Listen without judgment.

Day 17: Look up compound interest with a calculator.

Go to investor.gov/financial-tools-calculators. It's the SEC's free compound interest calculator. Plug in $50 a month, 7% annual return, starting at your current age. See what 40 years does to that number.

Day 18: Learn the difference between a Roth IRA and a traditional IRA.

Spend 15 minutes on this. The short version: Roth uses after-tax money and grows tax-free. Traditional uses pre-tax money, and you pay taxes on withdrawal. For teenagers, Roth is almost always better because you're in a low tax bracket now.

Day 19: Research custodial accounts at Fidelity, Schwab, or Vanguard.

Read about what they are, how to open one, and what the minimum investment is. Talk to a parent or guardian about opening one. You don't have to do it today, but having the conversation plants a seed.

Day 20: Practice the 48-hour rule.

Identify something you've been wanting to buy. Don't buy it today. Write it down and the date. Come back in 48 hours and see if you still want it as badly.

Day 21: Rest and reflect.

How is your relationship with money changing? What feels different from how it did three weeks ago? Write three sentences. This is progress.

Week 4: Share and Commit

Day 22: Teach someone one thing you've learned.

A friend, a sibling, anyone. Pick the one concept from this book that hit you hardest and explain it in your own words. You'll immediately know how well you understand it by whether you can explain it simply.

Day 23: Check your progress on your short-term goal.

Remember the goal you wrote on Day 14? How much have you saved toward it? Are you on track? If not, what's one thing you can adjust?

Day 24: Create a 'no-spend' challenge for yourself.

Pick 48 hours where you spend zero dollars on non-essentials. Document how it feels. Notice the moments when you're tempted. This isn't about deprivation; it's about building awareness.

Day 25: Write your personal money mission statement.

One or two sentences about what you want your financial life to look like and why. Something like: 'I want to never live paycheck to paycheck, so I'm building the habits now that make that impossible later.' Put it somewhere you'll see it.

Day 26: Look up one nonprofit or organization doing financial literacy work.

Besides Ten Cents of Hope, what else is out there? Junior Achievement, NFEC, Next Gen Personal Finance. Understanding the landscape helps you see where you fit and what gaps still need to be filled.

Day 27: Write a letter to your future self.

At 25. What do you want your financial situation to look like? What habits do you want to have built? What mistakes do you want to have avoided? Seal it or save it somewhere private. Read it again in five years.

Day 28: Share something from this book with someone who needs it.

Text a friend a concept. Post something on your story. Tell a sibling. Recommend the book. Plant a seed. This is what Ten Cents of Hope is actually about: the knowledge spreading outward.

Day 29: Review your month.

Go back through your tracking from the last 29 days. What did you learn? What changed? What stayed the same? Where do you want to be 30 days from now?

Day 30: Make a commitment.

Write down three habits you're committing to keep after this month: one around spending, one around saving, and one around learning. Sign it. Date it. Take a picture of it. Show someone. Committing to the public, even to just one person, dramatically increases the odds that you'll keep it.

That's it. Thirty days. You've tracked, built, learned, and shared. You've done more than most adults have ever done deliberately with their money. Now keep going.

Notes

V

Glossary

15

Commonly Used Terms In This Book

Financial words can sound complicated. They're not. Here's every key term from this book, explained in plain language.

Budget

A plan for how you'll use your money. Not a restriction, but a decision made in advance so you're in control instead of your money being in control.

Compound Interest

Earning interest on your interest. When your money earns a return, that return also starts earning a return. Over decades, this turns small amounts into large ones. Einstein reportedly called it the eighth wonder of the world.

Credit Score

A number (usually between 300 and 850) that represents how responsibly you've managed borrowed money. Higher is better. It affects whether you can rent an apartment, get a loan, or sometimes even get a job.

Custodial Account

An investment account opened by an adult on behalf of a minor. The adult manages it until the minor turns 18 (or 21 in some states), at which point it transfers fully to them. A great way for teenagers to start investing legally.

Debt

Money you owe to someone else. Not automatically bad; it's a tool. Debt used for education, housing, or productive investment can build wealth. Debt used for consumption (credit cards, buy-now-pay-later) without a repayment plan can trap you.

Dollar-Cost Averaging

Investing a fixed amount on a regular schedule regardless of what the market is doing. When prices are low, your fixed amount buys more. When prices are high, it buys less. Over time, this smooths out volatility and removes the pressure of trying to time the market.

ETF (Exchange-Traded Fund)

A basket of investments (like stocks) that you can buy as a single unit. Similar to an index fund but traded on the stock market throughout the day. Low cost, easy to start with small amounts, and highly diversified.

FAFSA

Free Application for Federal Student Aid. A form you fill out to apply for federal financial aid for college, including grants, loans, and work-study programs. One of the most important and most overlooked financial tools available to students from all income levels.

Index Fund

A fund that tracks a market index like the S&P 500, which includes the 500 largest American companies. Instead of trying to beat the market by picking individual stocks, you own a small piece of all of them. Low fees, broad diversification, and historically strong long-term returns.

Interest Rate

The percentage charged on borrowed money (when you're the borrower) or paid on saved/invested money (when you're the lender or investor). High interest rates on debt are expensive. High interest rates on savings are valuable.

Loss Aversion

A psychological bias where losing something feels roughly twice as painful as gaining the same thing feels good. Explains why people hold onto losing investments too long, avoid necessary risks, and make emotional rather than rational financial decisions.

Roth IRA

A retirement account where you contribute money you've already paid taxes on. It grows tax-free, and withdrawals in retirement are also tax-free. Ideal for teenagers and young adults who are currently in low tax brackets.

S&P 500

An index that tracks the 500 largest publicly traded companies in the United States. Often used as a benchmark for the overall health of the stock market. A long-term investment in an S&P 500 index fund has historically returned an average of about 10% per year before inflation.

Ten-Cent Mindset

The core philosophy of this book. Small, consistent financial decisions—made deliberately and repeatedly—compound into meaningful outcomes over time. You don't need to start big. You need to start.

Utilization Rate

The percentage of your available credit that you're currently using. If your credit card limit is $1,000 and you've charged $300, your utilization is 30%. Keeping this below 30% is one of the most important factors in maintaining a healthy credit score.

Notes

About the Author

Nihar Hari is a high school student and pianist from Apex, North Carolina. He wrote Ten Cents of Hope at sixteen, driven by a simple observation: the financial system touches every part of adult life, and almost no one explains how it works to the people who need to know before they're already in it.

Nihar is the founder of Ten Cents of Hope, a 501(c)(3) nonprofit organization dedicated to building financial literacy among youth. The nonprofit was born from the same question that runs through this book: what would change if young people understood money before the stakes were high?

Outside of his work with Ten Cents of Hope, Nihar is an accomplished pianist who has performed at Carnegie Hall's Weill Recital Hall. He is also a taekwondo practitioner, a volunteer with the Durham Veterans Affairs Medical Center, and a student who believes deeply that the skills that matter most are rarely the ones taught in class.

You can connect with me on:

- https://tencentsofhope.org
- https://www.linkedin.com/in/nihar-hari-98940830b
- https://www.instagram.com/tencentsofhope

Notes

www.ingramcontent.com/pod-product-compliance
Lightning Source LLC
LaVergne TN
LVHW021114300926
849160LV00009B/732
9798996565009